BUILDING A NAS SERVER WITH RASPBERRY PI AND OPENMEDIAVAULT

BRIAN SCHELL

Building a NAS Server with Raspberry Pi and Openmediavault

Copyright 2020 by Brian Schell.

Raspberry Pi, openmediavault, and other products mentioned within are trademarks owned by their respective companies. This book is not affiliated in any way with any group mentioned.

Written and designed by: Brian Schell
brian@brianschell.com

ISBN: 9798632268356
Version Date: March 31, 2020

CONTENTS

INTRODUCTION

WHAT DOES THIS BOOK COVER?

Put simply, this book covers all the steps necessary to build and configure a basic Network Attached Storage system using a Raspberry Pi and one or more hard drives. We'll look at buying and assembling a Raspberry Pi, how to download, install, and configure the Linux operating system, and how to download, install and configure the basic Openmediavault server software. All of this assumes you've never touched a Raspberry Pi or Linux before; it's a step-by-step book for non-techies.

We then look at two basic hardware configuration types: One with a single hard drive and the other with a dual-drive RAID setup, both of which can be expanded and customized quite a bit.

On the more advanced side, we will *not* be looking at Openmediavault plugins or Docker containers, as these are so specialized they simply aren't necessary for a basic NAS system. This is not an advanced configuration manual, nor does it cover every single option in the Openmediavault software. It's *what you need to know*, and *only* what you need to know to get yourself a reliable, working, inexpensive NAS setup!

Note that there a bazillion steps involved in configuring a NAS (only a mild exaggeration). If at some point, you get lost or think you may have missed something, skip ahead to the "Troubleshooting Checklist" chapter, where all the steps are laid out for you in a more basic form. If you accidentally skipped something, this list should be of help in tracking it down.

WHAT IS A NAS SERVER?

First things first, NAS stands for "Network Attached Storage," and it is just what it sounds like. It's storage (hard drives) for your files that are attached to a network. Instead of simply plugging an external or internal hard drive into your working computer, you have essentially a file server located somewhere in your home or office that offers access to files for any device on the premises, taking into account security settings that you can set up. This file server does nothing except act as a go-between between the network and the hard drives. Since this task is fairly light, processor-wise, a simple computer like a Raspberry Pi is just perfect for the task.

The software we will be installing to make this happen is called Openmediavault, or OMV for short. It's an open source project that is heavily developed and still getting new features regularly. It also allows new functions to be added via a plugin feature. OMV is the NAS software, but it all runs on the Linux operating system, which means it's stable and very reliable, not to mention all this software is completely free of charge.

WHAT IS A RASPBERRY PI?

This product with a silly name is actually a pocket-sized computer. This little box that fits in your pocket is as powerful as any computer you could buy ten years ago. That doesn't sound particularly impressive, but considering the tiny size and price of the Pi, it really is. Although you can set up a spare full-sized computer as your NAS server, a Raspberry Pi (RPI) is more than good enough for this project, and the whole system, bought new with everything you need, will only run you around $55, so it's much less expensive than buying a full-sized computer; probably even cheaper than buying most used PCs.

This book will focus on setting up a Raspberry Pi computer, installing and configuring the hard drive(s) and the Openmediavault software on it, and getting your files into the new system.

WHAT'S THE CATCH?

Well, the "tricky part" is that the Raspberry Pi computer runs Linux rather than Windows or MacOS, so it may require some learning to set up and use. That's the point of this book: to get you from knowing absolutely nothing about Linux or the Raspberry Pi to having a fully-working OMV file server.

IS THIS SAFE?

This was my number one consideration before attempting this project. In my own case, I have been collecting data and digital files since the 90s, and many of them are irreplaceable. I was a little skeptical about trusting a pocket-sized computer that costs under $55 to manage all that important data.

That said, all that is stored on the Raspberry Pi itself is the operating system and the basic OMV system files. All your data will be stored on regular, commercially-available hard drives of your choosing. Not only that, but I will be showing you how to set up hard drives in a RAID pair, so everything is duplicated, synchronized, and checked for any kind of corruption. Towards the end of the book, we'll also look at how to do a manual backup of the NAS drives so that you can do an off-site backup.

If your house burns down someday, you'll still lose your data, but otherwise, it's *no less* secure than storing your data on your computer. And with a proper regimen of backups, it'll be a whole lot safer. The convenience of having all your stuff in one place is worth the effort. Andrew Carnegie once said, "Put all your eggs in one basket, and then watch the basket." The man never saw a computer in his life, but his advice still applies here.

REQUIRED HARDWARE

OK, that all sounds good, so what do we need to buy to make this work? Not so much, really. You can go two ways.

RASPBERRY PI 4 SYSTEM:

- Raspberry Pi Model 4 system board ($35-$55 depending on RAM size)
- Some kind of enclosure or case made for the model 4 system ($6 and up)
- 5.1V / 3.0A DC output power supply with micro-USB plug ($8)
- Micro SD Card with 16GB capacity or more ($6)

RASPBERRY PI 3B+ SYSTEM:

- Raspberry Pi Model 3B+ system board (under $35)
- 3.5A Power supply with micro-USB plug ($7)
- Micro SD Card with 16GB capacity or more ($6)

- Some kind of enclosure or case made for the 3B+ system ($6 and up)

AND ALSO, FOR EITHER SYSTEM:

- An ethernet cable
- A PC or Mac computer that can access the SD Card for setup
- Up to four externally-powered hard drives to hold media files.

HARD DRIVE NOTES

Hard drive deals change regularly, so I'm not going to go into a lot of specifics here, but for the system I built for this book, I bought three identical external hard drives, the **Seagate Expansion Desktop 8TB External Hard Drive with USB 3.0**. Something similar would be fine. Obviously, I would recommend steering clear of too-cheap no-name brands. Reliability is completely dependent on the hard drives you use.

We're going to use two of these drives for the RAID storage, and the third will be used for our off-site backup, so you really only need two drives to get set up. If you don't really want to use RAID, then even a single drive can work fine; we'll look at both methods a little later.

The drives do need to be of the external variety, and moreover, need to be **powered** externally. The Raspberry Pi is a *very* low power device, and it simply cannot power even a single large hard drive through USB. The power needs to come from somewhere else. If you are going to use an SSD for your storage, that *may* be able to be powered from the Pi's USB-- your mileage may vary.

...And of course, the bigger the drive, the better.

RASPBERRY PI NOTES:

Let's start with the Pi. The current model of Raspberry Pi, as of this writing, is the Raspberry Pi 4. The 3B+ was the version available immediately before the 4 came out. Either of these will work for this project, but I would strongly recommend against going with anything older than these two models.

The model 4 Pi has several enhancements over the model 3B+ that make it a much better choice for serving files. The older models shared a single data bus for both the ethernet and USB systems, so reading or writing files over the network would be slowed as the devices had to share the bus. Since file transfer speed is one of the most important factors for a NAS, this is something to take into consideration. In addition, the 3B+ board is only available with 1MB of RAM, but the model 4 has options for 1MB, 2MB, or 4MB of RAM. The extra RAM options for the model 4 are not crucial, but here too, it may help speed things along.

My best recommendation is that unless you already have a model 3B+ sitting around gathering dust, just go with the model 4 system. It's got a better system architecture for data transfer and the option of larger memory. You will be happier with the model 4.

CASE NOTES:

The Pi 3B+ and 4 are not the same size or shape, so they require different cases. A cheap case for either can run as low as six dollars. With the 3B+, a cheap case is probably fine, as this model doesn't heat up very much. On the other hand, the model 4 is known for running very hot, and it's almost a necessity to get a case with a built-in fan or some kind of enhanced heat sink. My preferred case for either model is the **Flirc case**, available at most retailers that carry Pi accessories for around $16. The benefit of this case is that it's all-aluminum, and the case itself acts as one big heat sink. With a heat sink, there are no moving parts to wear out and no break-downs to worry about. They just work, reliably and for the long-term.

POWER SUPPLY NOTES:

The power supply for the 3B+ is essentially the same as an Android phone charger. It uses the micro-USB interface and the same voltage as an Android phone, so you may already have a charger that works with the Pi, or maybe not, since some phones may not have the necessary wattage. The Pi model 4 uses a power supply with a USB-C type connector. Either way, it's probably safest to simply purchase the dedicated power supply made for the Pi for around 7 or 8 dollars.

MICROSD CARD NOTES:

The MicroSD Card is what the Raspberry Pi uses to hold the operating system and the Openmediavault software. The operating system and OMV software can easily fit (minimally) on an 8GB card, but the data files that OMV uses need space, so I would recommend getting at least a 16GB ($6) or larger card. Personally, I started with a 16GB card, and I don't foresee a need to go bigger than that. The Pi will use the MicroSD card to boot and load the OMV software, but not for much else, so the speed rating of the card doesn't matter very much; at worst, a slow MicroSD card cause the operating system to take a few seconds longer to boot up.

ALSO NEEDED FOR SETUP:

In order to set everything up in the beginning, you'll need a working computer that has a port, adapter, or dongle that can read and write to the MicroSD Card you are going to use. You'll download the operating system, write it to the MicroSD card, and then use that card in the Pi. Once you've done this, you don't need the other computer anymore.

Surprisingly enough, you do **not** need a mouse, keyboard, or monitor for the Raspberry Pi. We are going to set this up entirely "headless." Once you assemble all the pieces, you can store the system in some out-of-the-way location that has access to power and ethernet, and then you're going to forget all about the hardware.

SETTING UP THE DEVICES

DOWNLOAD SOFTWARE IMAGE

Initially, we'll need to download the operating system software and install it on the MicroSD card. This will require a separate computer running Windows, Mac, or Linux. If you really can't make that work, there are many places that will sell you a preloaded MicroSD card with the software already installed; a simple Google search for "MicroSD Card Raspnian" will help you find a source in your country.

You will need a MicroSD Card and an adaptor/dongle to fit the card into whatever slot your computer has.

There are many distributions, or "brands" of Linux that are easily available. Two of the most popular for the Raspberry Pi are *Raspbian* and *Ubuntu*. Both of these focus on different things: Raspbian is the "official" operating system of the Raspberry Pi. Ubuntu, on the other hand, is a much heavier, more full-featured operating system that runs well on desktop systems and professional servers. Raspbian is faster and more efficient on the Pi, while Ubuntu is a bit more standardized with professionals and includes more built-in software, but it is also slower. For this project, simpler and faster is best, so we are going to use the Raspbian version here.

RASPBIAN:

Raspbian is released on an irregular schedule whenever enough changes accumulate. The latest version, as of this writing, is called "Buster" (February of 2020). If you want the cutting edge, most "official" version of the Raspberry Pi operating system, this is the one to use.

Raspbian can be found at

```
https://www.raspberrypi.org/downloads/raspbian/
```

NOTE ON WHICH VERSION TO DOWNLOAD:

You will see on Raspbian's download page that they offer three different versions:

- Raspbian Buster with desktop and recommended software
- Raspbian Buster with desktop
- Raspbian Buster Lite

Of course, by the time you read this, "Buster" may have been replaced by something newer. Still, three versions will be offered. The difference between the three versions lies in how much software you end up getting, and you can see the download sizes (on the website, but not shown here because they vary almost monthly) decrease for each of these three options. The first version is a full desktop experience, with a user interface like Windows and Mac, including a web browser, office software, etc. The middle version gives you the same basic desktop, but leaves out the office software, and the third version is a scaled-down, text-only operating system that looks like an "old-timey" Unix system.

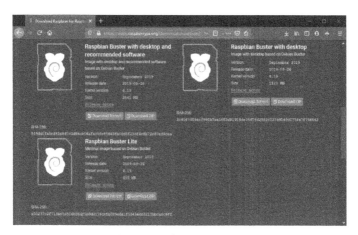

Three versions of Raspbian Available

The truth is, any of these versions will work fine, but if your Pi is going to be a dedicated file server and do nothing else, the smallest one, the third option, would be most efficient. There's less to keep updated, less chance of a bug creeping in, and less space used. If you know of some reason to go the full desktop route, then go ahead, but if not, then use the "Lite" version. The remainder of the book will discuss the Lite version, but the steps should be the same on all of them-- it's just that the "bigger" versions add stuff that we don't need for a file server and could slow the system down, at least slightly.

BURN TO SD CARD

Balena Etcher

The next piece of software that we'll need is a special utility to copy the operating system to the MicroSD Card and make it bootable. If you've copied files onto SD cards before, you might be wondering why this step is necessary. It's because this SD card must be bootable into a new operating system, which is more complicated than simply copying the files onto the card. The easiest application I've found to do this is **Balena Etcher**, usually just referred to as Etcher. There are versions available for Windows, Mac, and Linux, so wherever you're coming from, they make a version for you.

Balena Etcher can be found at:

```
https://www.balena.io/etcher/
```

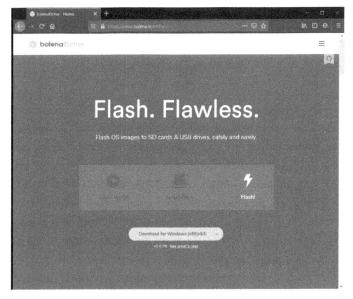

Balena's Website

Note: It is also possible to create an SD card image from the command line from MacOS or Linux, but it is complex, and actually impossible from Windows. For the sake of maximum compatibility and simplicity, I'm going to stick with using Etcher here, since it looks and works the same on all three major systems. If you simply *must* do it from the command line for some reason, the official documentation can be found here:

```
https://www.raspberrypi.org/documenta-
tion/installation/installing-
images/README.md
```

The process of creating a bootable MicroSD card with Etcher is simple once you have the above ingredients. If you downloaded Raspbian in the previous section, then you ended up downloading one large **.zip** file.

Once that's done, launch Etcher:

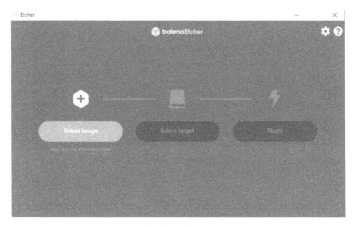

Etcher in Action

There are three buttons and icons. Click the one on the left, and it will allow you to choose a disk image. This is the single large Raspbian (or Ubuntu) file you just finished downloading.

Insert a MicroSD card into the computer. You may need

to use an adaptor, dongle, or hub to make it fit; this depends on your machine. Once the computer recognizes the card, click on Etcher's middle icon to select the card. **Make absolutely sure not to select the wrong disk, as you can delete your computer's hard drive if you aren't careful!** Make sure the description of the drive looks right and also compare the drive's reported size to what you think it is. Note that anything on the SD card will be erased in this process, so back up anything that's on there that you wish to save.

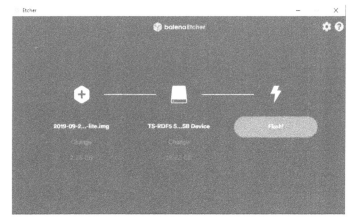

Ready to Flash the MicroSD Card

When you're done selecting the operating system file and the target drive, then click on the third icon, labeled "Flash!" This will begin the process of formatting the MicroSD Card and copying the operating system onto it. This process may take five to ten minutes depending on how fast your computer is, how fast the card is, and so forth.

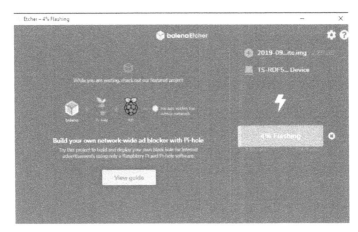

In Progress

Once the process has completed, Etcher will tell you that it has flashed the card successfully, or perhaps it will give you an error message. If there's an error, follow Etcher's suggestions to figure out what the problem is.

Done Creating MicroSD Card

You are done flashing the card, but do not eject the card yet, as there is one more step.

PREPARING THE SYSTEM FOR REMOTE ACCESS

You *could* now plug the Raspberry Pi into a keyboard and monitor and configure it locally, like a regular desktop computer. On the other hand, we plan to run the file server "headless," that is, out of the way somewhere without a monitor. If we plan to use it without a monitor in the long run, why not configure it the same way?

In order to access the operating system in order to install the OMV software, we need to set the Pi up for remote access. This is easiest to do from the same computer you used to burn the MicroSD card.

From Mac or Windows:

1. Make sure the MicroSD card is still inserted in the computer.
2. Open up a text editor app. On Mac, you can use the **Textedit** app, and on Windows, you use **Notepad**. These apps come with the operating system, so you do have them.
3. Create a new, blank file using the text editor.
4. Save it in the root folder of the MicroSD card. Use the filename "**ssh**"
5. Check to make sure it really saved it as **ssh** with no file extension. Depending on your settings, your text editor might append a .txt extension on the end. This file must have *no* extension. If the file has a .txt extension, then rename it to just plain *ssh* without that extension.
6. That's all. You just need to ensure that this little empty file exists in the main folder of the bootup

MicroSD card. When the operating system boots up for the first time, it will see that this file exists and enable the ability to access the computer remotely.

Assuming the process worked, you can eject the card from your PC and proceed to assembling your Pi.

ASSEMBLING THE PI HARDWARE

Assuming you have purchased or scrounged all the necessary pieces, assembling the Raspberry Pi is very easy, as it should be obvious from looking at the various ports where all the cables should go.

1. Insert your Raspberry Pi motherboard into your case and assemble it using whatever instructions come with the case you have chosen. If your case came with some form of heat sink, be careful not to get fingerprints on either the top of the processor or the bottom of the heat sink and use any thermal compound that came with the set. If it includes a fan, hook up the wires as instructed.
2. Slide the MicroSD Card (with the operating system already installed per the previous section) into the slot on the underside of the Raspberry Pi.
3. Do NOT plug in the hard drives yet. We'll get all the software set up first.
4. Plug in the ethernet cable between your Pi and your router. Note that Wi-Fi is vastly slower than a cabled connection, and I strongly discourage using Wi-Fi for this project. Either way, you will need a wired connection for the initial setup.

5. Plug the Raspberry Pi power adaptor into the wall outlet as well.

6. The final step, after everything else, is to plug the power supply into the Pi. The Raspberry Pi itself does not have a power switch, so applying power will start the boot process immediately. If your power supply *does* come with a switch or button, then turn it on now.

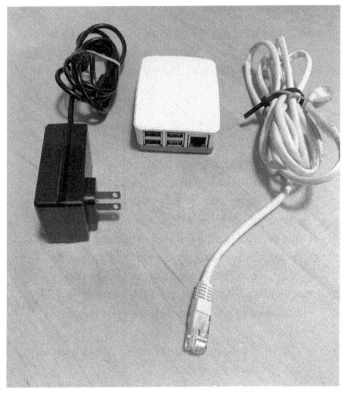

The Raspberry Pi Hardware. Pi, Case, Power Supply, and Ethernet cable.

At this point, You have a Raspberry Pi in a case with a heatsink and/or a fan. The Pi has a power supply and is plugged into your network. The MicroSD card is plugged in and set up with Raspbian (and includes the ssh file that we made manually). When the power comes on, you should see the Pi's red and green indicator lights come on and start blinking randomly. It's alive!

The Pi will do some configuration routines and first-time boot-up setup procedures, which may take a couple of minutes the very first time. Give the Pi a couple of minutes to get set up, and then proceed to the next section.

USING YOUR RASPBERRY PI REMOTELY

As I mentioned, most people run their OMV Server "head-less," that is, with no monitor or keyboard attached. This makes typing commands a bit of a challenge!

Not really, because we have already set the Pi up to be able to be accessed from other computers-- or even your smartphone. Keep in mind that if you find this procedure inconvenient for some reason, or if the process "breaks" someday, then you always have the option of plugging a keyboard and screen into your Pi and configuring it like a regular desktop computer.

You added that little empty ssh file onto your MicroSD card a while back, and that's going to let us get into the Pi and control it from other computers on the network. All we need on the other computer is a terminal app:

TERMINAL APPS TO USE:

- Windows: Download the app **Putty** from `https://putty.org/`

- Mac or Linux: Use the built-in *Terminal App*
- Android or iPhone: use the **Termius App** (See Google Play or IOS App Store)
- iPad: **Termius** or **Blink Shell App** (See App Store)

There are many other possible apps, but these are the ones I have used and am familiar with; others are probably just as good. If you are trying to find an app somewhere, search for a "SSH Terminal app" of some sort.

You will open up one of these terminal apps on your "main" computer and then use it to connect it to your Pi and type in commands that way. Note that this process is only for configuring and updating your system later-- you can use a much simpler OMV web interface to access your files and configuration settings, which we'll get to later. Download and install one of the above terminal apps on your regular computer or smartphone.

The first thing you need to know is the address on the network of the Raspberry Pi. Networking addresses are known as IP numbers, and for example, look like four numbers separated by periods: 192.168.0.1. There are two ways to find out what the address of your Pi is:

THE FIRST OPTION: LOOK AT YOUR ROUTER.

You will need to log into the configuration screen for your router and find the device's IP address. Every router is different, but most commonly, you can type http://192.168.0.1 into the URL bar in your browser to get there. If this doesn't bring up your router's login screen, you are going to need to refer to the instructions for your specific router (or skip to the second option, below).

After entering your router's username and password, you

can look at the menus to find the "DHCP Client List" somewhere. Look at the list of devices shown, and figure out
which IP address has been assigned to the Raspberry Pi. This
is a hassle to do every time you want to change a setting, so
it's a good idea to assign a permanent IP number to your Pi.
Again, check the documentation for your router on how to
do this.

You can find the IP number in the administration screen of your router.

My router as an example. Yours WILL vary.

From the picture, you can see that my Raspberry Pi's IP
Number is 192.168.0.4, and that I have it set there
permanently.

Note on IP address reservation: It is important that
you use your router's settings to make sure that it assigns the
SAME IP NUMBER to the Raspberry Pi every time it boots
up. It's not absolutely crucial, but it is extremely convenient
to always know where to find your file server without having
to find an IP number each time. The procedure to do this
varies from router to router, so I cannot walk you through
this, but in my screenshot above, the option following
"DHCP Clients List" is "Address Reservation." You will need

to click "Add Reservation" and then enter the Raspberry Pi's **MAC address** and the **IP number** you want to reserve. Both of these numbers can be seen in the DHCP Client List. Again, check your router's documentation if necessary.

All those other devices have IPs that are assigned "randomly" as they boot up, but once reserved, the Raspberry Pi will always be found at 192.168.0.4.

SECOND OPTION: DOWNLOAD AN IP SCANNER

This requires yet another download and install, but it's a useful tool to have. It's called *Angry IP Scanner*, and it's a free security tool that lists everything on your network. You can download it for Windows, Mac, or Linux from:

```
https://angryip.org/
```

Angry IP Scanner startup screen

The above image is the startup screen for Angry IP Scanner. It's fine to just click next until the introductory screens go away. Once the app has gone through all the explanations, you should just be able to hit the "Start" button to make the magic happen:

	IP Range - Angry IP Scanner		
IP Range: 192.168.0.0	to 192.168.0.255	IP Range	
Hostname: Brians-iMac.local	IP↑ Netmask	Start	

IP	Ping	Hostname	Ports [0+]
192.168.0.4	0 ms	raspberrypi.local	[n/s]
192.168.0.5	0 ms	Brians-iMac.local	[n/s]
192.168.0.7	1 ms	Living-Room.local	[n/s]
192.168.0.1	0 ms	[n/a]	[n/s]
192.168.0.2	1 ms	[n/a]	[n/s]
192.168.0.17	0 ms	Brians-iMac.local	[n/s]
192.168.0.20	0 ms	Kevins-MacBook-Pr...	[n/s]

Ready   Display: All   Threads: 0

Results of Angry IP Scanner

And as you can see in the image above, the Angry IP Scanner has scanned my network and now shows the active devices and their IP numbers. The number for the Raspberry PI is very easy to determine this way. It's 192.168.0.4 on my network.

Write this number down, as you'll need it any time you want to update the Openmediavault software or the underlying operating system.

Whew! Now we're ready to begin actually accessing the Pi.

From the terminal app you installed on your computer or other device, type:

```
ssh pi@192.168.0.4
```

be sure to substitute whatever your IP address is for mine. Depending on the terminal app you downloaded, you may need to navigate a menu or fill in some blanks to enter the IP number.

The default user name is "pi" and the password "raspberry." Once you connect to the system, you will be at a command prompt on the Pi itself, which should look similar to this:

```
blink> ssh pi@192.168.0.4
Ed25519 key fingerprint is SHA256:ZW+29guimEOvONBw9eYsrDLaKVel2EpbbxWWeRMoUo4.
The server is unknown.
Do you trust the host key? (yes/no): yes
This new key will be written on disk for further usage.
Do you agree? (yes/no): yes
Password:
Linux raspberrypi 4.19.97-v7l+ #1294 SMP Thu Jan 30 13:21:14 GMT 2020 armv7l

The programs included with the Debian GNU/Linux system are free software;
the exact distribution terms for each program are described in the
individual files in /usr/share/doc/*/copyright.

Debian GNU/Linux comes with ABSOLUTELY NO WARRANTY, to the extent
permitted by applicable law.

SSH is enabled and the default password for the 'pi' user has not been changed.
This is a security risk - please login as the 'pi' user and type 'passwd' to set a new password.

Wi-Fi is currently blocked by rfkill.
Use raspi-config to set the country before use.

pi@raspberrypi:~ $
```

You have logged into the Raspberry Pi!

Typing commands here are executed on the Raspberry Pi, not your local computer; it's like using your device as a remote keyboard and monitor!

FIRST-TIME RASPBIAN SETUP

Eventually, you will wind up at the Raspbian login screen:

```
Raspbian GNU/Linux 10 raspberrypi tty1
raspberrypi login: _
```

The default user for the system is:

Login/Username = **pi**
Password = **raspberry**

Once you have logged in, you should end with a welcome message and a blinking Linux command prompt:

```
Linux raspberrypi 4.19.97-v71+ #1294 SMP
Thu Jan 30 13:21:14 GMT 2020 armv71

The programs included with the Debian
GNU/Linux system are free software; the
exact distribution terms for each program
```

```
are described in the individual files in
/usr/share/doc/*/copyright.

Debian GNU/Linux comes with ABSOLUTELY NO
WARRANTY. to the extent permitted by
applicable law.

pi@raspberrypi: $
```

Your operating system is now installed. Now it's time to get it usable!

CHANGING THE PASSWORD FOR THE PI USER

The first thing we need to do is deal with a basic security issue. First, we will change the password for the default user. As mentioned above, the default is user **pi** and that user's password is **raspberry**. Since this is the same username and password for *every* default Raspbian install, it's a very good idea to change the password. This user has superuser access and has the ability to delete and change literally anything, so make the password something hard to guess.

At the command prompt, type

```
passwd
```

and follow the prompts. The initial password is "raspberry," but for your new password, you can enter just about anything.

We're going to install the Openmediavault server as the user "pi," so we don't need to add any users right now.

Also, we need to be able to log into the Pi using the "Root Administrator" and be able to change system files that way. To enable this, type:

```
sudo adduser pi ssh
```

This adds the user 'pi' to the system group *ssh*, allowing this access.

[Optional] If, for some reason, you do want to add more users, you can use the command:

```
adduser
```

and follow the prompts. The only required fields for this command are the new person's username and the password. Again, for a basic file server, you don't need additional Linux users. You can have multiple users for your file server, but that's done later.

UPDATING THE SYSTEM

It's time to ensure that everything is up-to-date on your system. I know-- you just downloaded it, so how could you have out-of-date software already? Raspbian only updates their big "distribution" files every few months, but the individual apps are changed and updated as the need arises. Updating is an easy, two-step process. Type:

```
sudo apt update
```

Note that if you get a bunch of error messages then something is wrong. Wait a minute or two and try again-- it could be something goofy out on the Internet. If the problem persists, then something is probably wrong with your ethernet connection. Shutdown the system by typing

```
sudo shutdown -h now
```

and the system will shut down. Unplug it and plug it back in to reboot. You may need to reset your router as well, but that's unusual.

Assuming everything works, then the `sudo apt update` command will go out on the Internet and download a list of all the files that make up your system and compare that list to what you have installed. Anything that is newer on the list gets marked for upgrading in the next step. When the "update" command is done, then type:

```
sudo apt upgrade
```

This command looks at that "update" list and then goes through and downloads and installs everything that has newer versions available. It's a very smart and useful system, and (unlike Windows) you only do it *when you are ready* for updates.

And that's it-- We bought and assembled all the pieces, and then we downloaded and created our boot media. We then set up Wi-Fi, changed our password, updated the system, and ended up with a bare-bones, but still fully working little computer. Keep in mind that since we are "only" building a file server, we chose the command-line server version of Raspbian. We could have chosen the full desktop version and run the Raspberry Pi as a low-powered computer with office software, web browsing, and everything. Or maybe that can be your project for another time...

INSTALLING OPENMEDIAVAULT

DOWNLOADING AND INSTALLING OMV

And we're finally ready to install OMV by typing ALL of the following in one big, long line:

```
wget -O - https://github.com/OpenMedia-
Vault-Plugin-Developers/install-
Script/raw/master/install | sudo bash
```

Note that the first part reads "wget -O(capital letter "O" not zero) space hyphen space https…"

A bunch of installation messages will fill your screen and probably scroll for several pages. There's a lot of messages, and the installation will probably take 15-30 minutes. As long as stuff keeps appearing on the screen, let it run.

Assuming nothing goes wrong, we will eventually get the message:

"It is recommended to reboot and then setup the network

adapter in the openmediavault web interface," letting us know that OMV is installed.

The final step is to verify our IP address, by typing:

```
ifconfig
```

at the command prompt, and make note of the Raspberry Pi's IP address. The output from ifconfig will look like this:

```
wlan0: flags=4163<UP,BROADCAST,RUNNING,MUL-
TICAST> mtu 1500
inet 192.168.0.4 netmask 255.255.255.0
broadcast 192.168.0.255
inet6 fe80::594f:cad3:ff2a:c07e prefixlen
64 scopeid 0x20<link>
ether dc:a6:32:02:b1:56 txqueuelen 1000
(Ethernet)
RX packets 52230 bytes 73794731 (70.3 MiB)
RX errors 0 dropped 0 overruns 0 frame 0
TX packets 24158 bytes 9006450 (8.5 MiB)
TX errors 0 dropped 0 overruns 0 carrier 0
collisions 0
```

The only part that matters is the beginning of the second line, right after "inet." This is your *IP address*, the numerical location for your RPI in the local network in your home or office. It's formatted as four numbers separated by periods. In the example above, the IP address for my Raspberry Pi system is **192.168.0.4**, and this is how I'll access OMV from now on. When you see this number elsewhere in the book, just remember to substitute your own number.

Now it's time to reboot the Pi and start configuring OMV. On the command line, type

```
sudo reboot
```

And give the system a minute or two to do the reboot. Meanwhile, we can load our web browser on our computer or on whatever device you're using.

COMMAND LINE/TERMINAL QUICK REFERENCE

Here are some reminders on the terminal commands to control your machine:

1. Accessing OMS from a terminal app on the same network: (Replace with your IP number):

ssh pi@192.168.0.4

2. If you need to shutdown or turn off the Pi server, type (in a terminal) :

sudo shutdown -h now

3. To reboot the system, then simply type (in a terminal):

sudo reboot

4. To upgrade the system software type these two commands:

sudo apt update
sudo apt upgrade

CONFIGURING OPENMEDIAVAULT

After giving the Raspberry Pi time to reboot, switch over to a web browser on your computer or some device that's on the same network as the Pi. Type the IP Number of the Pi into the URL bar in your browser and hit Enter. You should see the OMV Login window, like below:

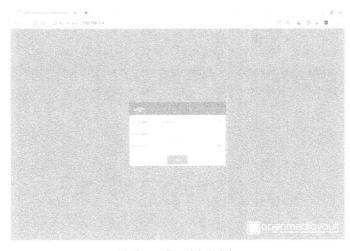

The Openmediavault login dialog

The username to type in (all lowercase) is: `admin`

The password to type in (all lowercase) is: `open-mediavault`

and you should soon see the main web administration screen for Openmediavault:

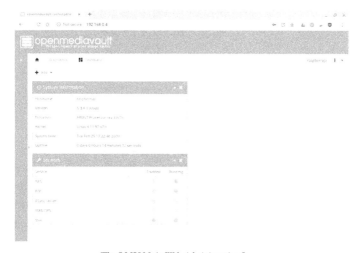

The OMV Main Web Administration Screen

At the far right, just to the right of the name "raspber-rypi" is the three-dot menu. If you click on this, you will see options to change the language used for OMV, as well as options to logout, reboot, standby, and shutdown.

- **Logout:** Logs off the user from the web interface.
- **Reboot:** Reboots the Raspberry Pi.
- **Standby:** Puts the OMV software into "Standby" mode, thereby making the system "hibernate."
- **Shutdown:** Does the same as `sudo shutdown -h now`, allowing you to power off or pull the plug on your equipment without the need to use a terminal app.

Note that you can use these options to **shutdown or reboot** the system instead of typing those commands into the command line through a terminal. This makes shutting down the system far easier!

Continuing on to the main interface, just under the blue "openmediavault" logo is a "home" logo. Just to the left of the home button is a small white arrow. Click that arrow to open the Settings pane:

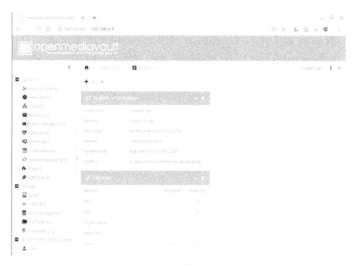

The Settings Pan (On the Left)

HOW TO CHANGE SETTINGS

This Settings pane is where we will configure most of the options within OMV.

One annoying thing about OMV is that it will log you out after only five minutes of inactivity. This will quickly drive you crazy, so let's change this behavior and in the process, learn how the settings screen works. Under the "System" section of the settings pane, find and click on the option for

"General Settings."

Right up at the top of the General Settings is an option to change the port and to change the auto logout. Don't change the port unless you know of some reason to do so, but **do** change the auto logout to something more convenient, say 30 minutes (use the pull-down menu and select the 30-minute option).

NOTHING you do in OMV will actually take effect until you click the "save" button near the top of the screen. This seems logical, but even after you click save, a yellow banner will pop up near the top of the window, telling you "The configuration has been changed. You must apply the changes in order for them to take effect." Then there are buttons for "Apply" and "Revert." Once you click on "Apply" you will often get another dialog, once again asking you to confirm your changes. These messages start to get annoying very quickly, and at some point, you'll probably have something not work, and you will eventually track it down to the fact that you forgot to click a confirmation somewhere. This is just something we'll have to deal with, as OMV doesn't want to do anything unless you are really certain about it, which is probably a good thing.

You'll soon be VERY acquainted with the yellow confirmation bar (at the top)

On that same main screen, beneath the home button, are tabs for "Web Administration" and "Web Administrator Password." Click on the second one to change the Administrator password. Be sure to click on "Save" to save the new password. Of all places to be different, **this** screen doesn't ask you for a confirmation.

CONFIGURING THE HARD DRIVE(S)

Now that we've set up the system and gotten OMV running, with a new Administrator password, we can start adding drives. We're going to look at two different drive configurations in this book:

1. A single SSD Drive.
2. A pair of two hard drives set up in a RAID 1 configuration.

Both of these are common setups, and you can mix and

match your hardware as needed; i.e. set up a single hard drive instead of an SSD or use two SSDs in a Raid system instead of the hardware. If you don't have any spare hard drives, you can even use flash drives or NVME drives. MOST forms of disk-type storage work just fine here.

Before plugging in a new drive (or any hardware devices), you should shut down your Raspberry Pi. To do this, go into your terminal program and connect like you did before. Once you have a command line, type

```
sudo shutdown -h now
```

Within a few seconds, the system will disconnect your terminal session and shutdown the operating system. If you've already access the Openmediavault web interface, you can much more conveniently shut down the system from there, using the "three-dot menu" in the upper-right portion of the web interface and choosing the option to **shutdown**.

Note that the Raspberry Pi does not shut off its own power. After the command above has completed, you'll need to unplug or otherwise switch off the Pi device. To reboot, just plug it back in. This is a somewhat clunky process, but you shouldn't need to shut down very often.

CONFIGURING A SINGLE SSD DRIVE

Let's start with the easiest configuration, a single drive.

In this example, I'm going to use a Samsung T5, 500-giga-byte SSB drive here, but any drive will work. This particular drive has the benefit of not needing external power, so the only cable is the one going to the Pi. Any non-SSD-type drive will need external power, but some SSDs are low-power enough to work without external power. That said, SSDs are generally pretty small to use in a file server, but it's something to think about if your storage needs are fairly modest.

A Very Common External SSD Drive, The Samsung T5

With the power disconnected from the Pi, plug in the drive. If your drive does need power, then plug it in, or turn it on, or whatever it needs. Finally, plug in/turn on the Raspberry Pi and give it a minute or two to boot up.

Now you can connect to the OMV server via a web browser with the IP number typed into the URL bar as before. This is how you will always access the OMV Settings and configuration information in the future, with the exception of doing software upgrades through the command line.

Bring up the Settings pane by clicking on the white arrow next to the home button. Look down the list and under "Storage," click on "Disks." You should see your disk drive appear after a few moments:

Storage -> Disks

In my screenshot above, you can see the first line is:

```
/dev/sda Portable SSD T5 S50TNV0M80...
Samsung 465.76 GiB
```

and the second line also has:

```
/dev/mmc... n/a n/a n/a 14.84 Gib
```

OK, so there are two drives attached to the system. As you might guess by the reported size, the second drive is the MicroSD card that holds the operating system. Never, *__ever__* do anything with this drive in OMV. Occasionally, there may be some reason that we will change the system on the MicroSD via the terminal app, but there's literally nothing in the web interface that should **ever** change the MicroSD card. That way lies destruction and suffering.

The first drive, on the other hand, is my Samsung SSD drive, which is the one I want to use. I have some old junk on that drive that I want to erase, so I will click on the line to highlight it and then click the "Wipe" button that appears just above the list. A confirmation will appear, and I choose "Yes." Next, comes a dialog that asks how I want to delete the disk:

1. **Secure** - Erases the information on the disk and overwrites the files with new data, forever destroying the original data and making it unrecoverable. In physical terms, think "Shredder." Note that Secure "shredding" can take quite a long time, maybe an hour or more for a large drive, so don't waste your time with this if you don't really need it.

2. **Quick** - Erases the information on the disk, but does so in a manner that might allow it to be recoverable by an expert. In physical terms, think "trash can." A quick erase only takes a couple of seconds.

3. **Cancel** - doesn't erase the disk

Choose the one that you want. For a new drive, a quick wipe is fine.

After wiping the drive, you need to create a file system on the drive. In the Settings pane, choose "Storage" and "File System." You'll see the information for the MicroSD card here, but not your wiped drive. That's because without a file system, the operating system cannot really "see" the drive. Click on the "Create" button above the list. This will bring up a "Create file system" control panel:

Create File System Dialog

If you pull down the dropdown list next to "Device," your wiped hard drive should appear. Select it from the list. The next box is called "Label." Make up a name to make it easier to identify the disk— I called mine SamsungSSD. Unless you know some reason to change it, leave the file system setting on EXT4.

Click on OK, and once again, you will get a confirmation box explaining that formatting will erase everything on your drive. This is normal, and since we *want* to start with a blank drive, that's a good thing. Click on "Yes," and your drive will be formatted. Depending on the size and speed of your drive, this may take several minutes. Again, watch the status window for any problems.

After a few minutes, the File System window will show you something like this:

The Completed File System

The next step is to click on your newly formatted drive to select it, then choose the "Mount" button, located above the list of drives. It may take a moment, but you'll soon get the yellow confirmation bar at the top. Click to proceed.

The drive is now set up and configured. Now we have to set up security and permissions to allow people to access the drive.

In the left column under "Access Rights Management" click "Shared Folders." In the beginning, you won't see anything in this list. Choose the "Add" button to bring up the "Add shared folder" dialog:

Add Shared Folder Dialog

In the "Name" field, you will need to think of a name for your shared folder. I used the not-so-creative name "Files" here. Under the "Device" field, you should be able to select your drive from the pull-down list. If you see a need to use a different folder/path name than "Files/" for your files, then you can change this in the third field.

The "Permissions" drop-down list offers a lot of choices. Look through the choices and choose the one that you need. For our example, I'm going to go with "Everyone: read/write." There are also options to restrict user's and non-user's reading and writing privileges, depending on the folder. We'll look at some of the other security options later, when we set up the second example (the RAID drives).

Once you have everything set as needed, click on "Save" and prepare to confirm your selections.

Now we have the drive set up. We have our security permissions set. All we need to do now is tell the computer how to let the user access the data remotely. Click on "Services" to enable various network access methods.

For an example, click on "SSH." SSH is already enabled for our server, as we used SSH to connect and do things on the command line via the terminal. I don't have any recommended changes for you, but if there are any specific settings you want to modify concerning ssh, you can do that here.

For a typical NAS, you should choose "SMB/CIFS." SMB stands for *Server Message Block*, and is a protocol for sharing files, printers, serial ports, and communications abstractions such as named pipes and mail slots between computers. Samba is an easy system to set up, and every operating system support it to some extent.

In the SMB configuration screen, the only thing you would have to do is "Enable" SMB with the first switch. Save your settings and confirm when the system asks. Of course, if you want to alter the other settings for your network or needs, then you can, but all I did was to flip to switch to enable SMB:

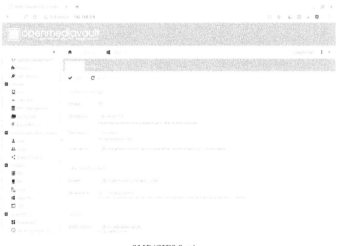

SMB/CIFS Settings

But we aren't finished with this screen yet. Click on the "Shares" tab just above the Save/Reset buttons. In the tab, click on "Add" to set up a SMB share. Click on the dropdown menu for "Device" to choose your hard drive and shared folder. Mine shows up as "Files [on SamsungSSD, Files/]".

Once the device is selected, make sure the "enabled" switch is green. Also, change the "Public" option to "Only Guests." The many other options here can mostly be ignored, unless you know of a reason to change something for your specific needs.

Creating a Share

Again, click Save and confirm after enabling, choosing the device, and allow guests only.

Now, when you look at the list of shares, you should see a big green dot next to your new, active, shared drive.

And that's it for the basic concepts of Openmediavault and setting up shared drives. Now, we'll look at how to create user account and set up password-based security for the file server.

SETTING UP MULTIPLE USERS AND SECURITY PASSWORDS

The above setup creates a single drive that is publically available to anyone who is on your network. This is fine for sharing your files (say music or family photos) with the whole family, but usually, most people want a secure place for all their files, and they don't want anyone else to have access.

This is not a difficult process with Openmediavault, but once again, it requires a number of steps:

1. First decide how many users you will have and what their usernames and passwords will be.

2. Under the Settings pane, click on "Access Rights Management" and "Users." Then use the "Add" button to create a user account for your first user. You'll need their real name, their username, a new password, and an email for each user. Create one user account for each person.

3. Under the Settings pane, click on "Access Rights Management" and "Groups." Then use the "Add" button to create a group for each user. Under the "General" tab, enter the name of the group, which should be the same as the user's name. Then, under the "Members" tab, click on the user name to be assigned to this account. First you create a user, then you create a group, then you assign that user to the group.

4. Under the Settings pane, click on "Access Rights Management" and "Shared folders." Then use the "Add" button to create a folder for that user. You will give the Share a name, then pull down the drive list and choose the hard drive. Lastly, you will type a Folder Name in the Path field. You will need to create a shared folder for each user. The following will create a shared folder named "Brian/" on the Samsung hard drive:

Access Right Management -> Shared Folders -> Add

5. Under the Settings pane, click on "Access Rights Management" and "Shared folders." Click to select one of the newly-created shares and then choose "Privileges" from the buttons above the list. Check the box to allow that user access to his own folder, but uncheck anything else. Choose "Save" and then confirm everything. Again, you must set privileges for each of the shared folders.

6. Under the Settings pane, click on "Shared folders," click one of the new shared folders and then click the "ACL" button. The bottom pane "Extra Options" are what we need to change here.

```
Owner: root: Read/Write/Execute
Groups: users: Read/Write/Execute
Others: Read/Execute
```

Change "Groups" to the appropriate username for that share. Change Others to "None." At the bottom, check both boxes (replace existing, apply to subfolders). Save and confirm your changes.

7. For the final step, under the Settings pane, click on

"Services" and "SMB/CIFS." Switch from the "Settings" tab to the "Shares" tab (in the bar above the "Save" button).

8. Highlight one of the shares and choose "Edit." Look at the various settings to see if they all look correct to you, but specifically, make sure that the "Inherit ACLs/Honor existing ACLs" switch is turned on. Then, of course, save and confirm.

And that should set up your users, the groups, and the folders they will use to store their files.

If you are only interested in setting up a single-drive system like the one we just did, then skip over the next section and go straight to "Connecting a Shared Drive." If you'd like to set up a dual-drive RAID system, then continue into the next chapter.

SETTING UP A DUAL-DRIVE RAID SYSTEM

RAID has a reputation of being more secure and safer than a single drive system. This is absolutely **not true**. There *is* redundancy in the case one of the drives fails, but there is no extra protection against getting a virus or malware. There is no safety net in case of a fire or flood. If someone steals your system, you will still lose everything. To solve these problems, you need a good backup and off-site storage plan. This could be an online system like Crashplan or Carbonite, or it could be as simple as taking a spare hard drive to your parent's house for storage.

That said, RAID is an interesting technology that does in fact, help protect against losing data when a hard drive fails. Then again, so does a good backup plan. If it sounds like I'm pushing you towards making regular and reliable backups, then good— that's what I'm doing!

OK then, let's get on with setting up our "Redundant Array of Inexpensive Disks," using Openmediavault to control everything. It's not really hard at all.

You will need:

1. The same Raspberry Pi with Raspbian and OMV installed as in the previous sections.
2. Two (or more) externally powered hard drives, as large as you can afford.
3. That's all!

Warning: With the process we are going to use, we will be formatting BOTH hard drives, so anything already on the drives will be lost. If you have a bunch of data to import, set up these two hard drives first, then add your current drive as a THIRD drive until you have copied over your data to the RAID system.

1. Power down and turn off the power to your Pi, then assemble and plug in the two external hard drives. Use whatever instructions came with the drive to plug in the USB cables and power supplies. It should be pretty obvious where to plug in the cables by looking at the ports on the back of the drives. Plug the USB cables into two or more ports on the Raspberry Pi. I would strongly advise against using any kind of hub or splitter or anything like that. For the best performance, plug them directly into the Pi. Since you are running the Pi "headless," there's probably nothing else in those USB ports anyway.

2. Next, power up the Pi and wait for it to boot. Once that's ready, you can go into the OMV Web interface, and click on "Disks" in the Settings pane, and you should see the two disks listed there.

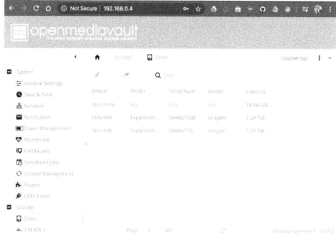

System -> Disks

The may have other names, but most likely, the Device names will be:

```
/dev/sda
/dev/sdb
```

Whatever you see for the Model, Serial Number, and size depends on the drives you have.

3. It ***seems logical*** that the next step would be to go to "Storage" and click on "RAID Management." Sure enough, there's a button there to "Create" new drives. If you were running OMV on a standard desktop computer, this would be fine. Instead, you get a message:

No External RAID Drives? What?

It says, "Select the devices that will be used to create the RAID device. Devices connected via USB will not be listed (too unreliable)." Well, that stinks, because that's exactly what we wanted to do! The simple fact is that fast, modern USB drives are not any less reliable than any other kind of drive. Some USB interfaces on older drives and computers can cause some slowdowns, but that's something we can live with. To get around this limitation will take a bit of typing in the terminal to set up the drives, but once that's done, it'll all work exactly as you would expect.

4. First, go to "Services" and click on "SMB/CIFS" in the Settings pane and click the "Enable" switch to TURN IT OFF. Then, with SMB *disabled*, click on "Save" and then confirm as usual. This service may take a few moments to shut down.

5. Start up your terminal app on your computer and connect to the OMV server in the usual way (*ssh*

pi@192.168.0.4). From the command line in your terminal app, type the following:

```
ls -l /dev/sd*
```

and when you hit enter, you should see a list something like this:

```
pi@raspberrypi:~ $ ls -l /dev/sd*
brw-rw---- 1 root disk 8, 0 Feb 28 11:31
/dev/sda
brw-rw---- 1 root disk 8, 1 Feb 28 11:31
/dev/sda1
brw-rw---- 1 root disk 8, 2 Feb 28 11:31
/dev/sda2
brw-rw---- 1 root disk 8, 16 Feb 28 11:31
/dev/sdb
brw-rw---- 1 root disk 8, 17 Feb 28 11:31
/dev/sdb1
brw-rw---- 1 root disk 8, 18 Feb 28 11:31
/dev/sdb2
```

This verifies that the two drives are plugged in and working correctly. There is, in fact, an sda and sdb drive. The lines for sda1 and sda2 are for partitions on those drives, and what you see with your drives will vary somewhat. **Still, you should see sda and sdb here**, if not the other things.

6. Still at the command prompt, type:

```
sudo mdadm --create /dev/md/name /dev/sda1
/dev/sdb1 --level=1 --raid-devices=2
```

all on one long line. When you hit enter, you will see some warnings:

```
pi@raspberrypi:~ $ sudo mdadm --create
/dev/md/name /dev/sda1 /dev/sdb1 --level=1
--raid-devices=2

mdadm: Note: this array has metadata at the
start and may not be suitable as a boot
device. If you plan to store '/boot' on
this device please ensure that your boot-
loader understands md/v1.x metadata, or use
--metadata=0.90
Continue creating array?
```

Type "yes" at this prompt and in a moment, you will see:

```
mdadm: Defaulting to version 1.2 metadata
mdadm: array /dev/md/name started.
```

7. If you go back to the web interface and click on "Storage" and "RAID Management," you will now see something like the following:

Storage -> RAID Management

If you watch the column "State," you will see that it is slowly resyncing the two drives. In the screenshot above, you can see that it says "735 minutes" to completion. This isn't really all that accurate, but this step <u>will</u> take a long time. Depending on the size of your drives, it may be more or less than mine. My example system, with two 8TB hard drives, took almost exactly ***eighteen hours*** to finish. Yes, this is a bit ridiculous, but this is the one, single major drawback of using a Raspberry Pi for this project. The RAID will run fine, but it takes a crazy amount of time to do the original sync between drives (it'd take a long time on any other system as well). Eventually, the "State" field will show as "clean."

8. Once the syncing finally finishes, click on "File Systems" and then select the new RAID drive that appears there. Note that it will not appear until after the syncing in the previous step is done. Click on "Create" and then use the Device pull-down menu to select the RAID device, "Software RAID raspberry pi" you just made. Do not choose the individual drives (sda or sdb). Create a name for the new drive. Leave the file system EXT4 unless you know of some reason to choose differently.

9. A dialog will appear confirming that you really want to

format the drive. Click to confirm that you do, and watch the next screen as the drive formats. This also will take some time, possibly a half-hour to an hour. After step 7 above, just one hour seems like an easy wait, doesn't it?

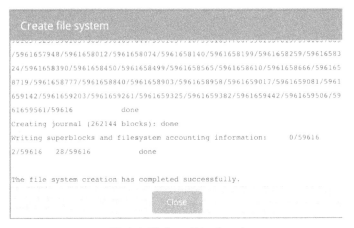

Watch the File System Being Created

10. Once the drive has been formatted, you can select the device, then click on "Mount" to mount the drive. You will need to confirm as usual.

11. Decide how many users for whom you want to create private folders.

12. Under the Settings pane, click on "Access Rights Management" and "Users." Then use the "Add" button to create a user account for your first user. You'll need their real name, their username, a new password, and an email for each user. Create one user account for each person.

13. Under the Settings pane, click on "Access Rights Management" and "Groups." Then use the "Add" button to create a group for each user. Under the "General" tab, enter the name of the group, which should be the same as the user's name. Then, under the "Members" tab, click on the user

name to be assigned to this account. First you create a user, then you create a group, then you assign that user to the group.

14. Go to "Access Right Management" and "Shared Folders." Click on "Add" to create a new share. Name the share anything you like, then use the drop-down menu to choose the RAID device. The name you just entered will auto-populate in the "Path" field, but you can change this path name if you prefer.

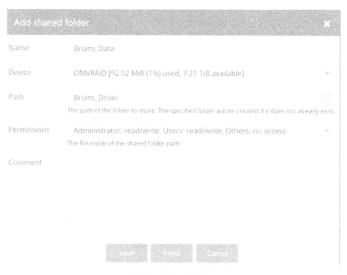

Adding a Shared Folder

15. Change the Permissions to whatever you want. For our example, I'm going to go with "Administrator: read/write, Users: read/write, Others: No access." Click on "Save" and then confirm as usual.

16. Repeat steps 12 through 15 for as many users as you will need. Each user gets his/her own shared folder. In the screenshot below, I have two shares, "Brians_Data" and "Kevins_Data" :

17. Under the Settings pane, click on "Access Rights Management" and "Shared folders." Click to select one of the newly-created shares and then choose "Privileges" from the buttons above the list. Check the box to allow that user access to his own folder (and group if necessary), but uncheck anything else. Choose "Save" and then confirm everything. Again, you must set privileges for each of the shared folders.

18. Under the Settings pane, click on "Shared folders," click one of the new shared folders and then click the "ACL" button. The fields in the bottom pane, "Extra Options" are what we need to change here; you can ignore the top panes of this dialog. The default values under "Extra options" are already set to:

```
Owner: root: Read/Write/Execute
Groups: users: Read/Write/Execute
Others: Read/Execute
```

Use the pull-down menu to change the "Group" to the appropriate group that matches the username for that share. Change "Others" to "None." At the bottom, check both boxes (replace existing permissions, apply to files and subfolders). Save and confirm your changes. Now, go back and repeat this step for each user account that you created earlier.

19. Under the Settings pane, click on "Services" and "SMB/CIFS." Turn on the switch for "Enable" under the General Settings section. Save and confirm.

20. Switch from the "Settings" tab to the "Shares" tab (in the bar above the "Save" button).

21. Click on "Add." Make sure the new share has "Enable" turned on, and then select the shared folder you want to acti-vate from the drop-down list. Unless you know of some reason to change the other settings, you can ignore the rest. Click on "Save" and then confirm.

22. Repeat step 21 until you have activated a share for each user.

23. ...and we're done! Now you can access and use the drive like any other network drive!

Next, we should look into how we actually log in, connect, and use this new NAS system!

CONNECTING TO A SHARED DRIVE ON THE NETWORK

You've got all that data on your NAS, or you soon will have, so how do you intend to access it? This section shows how to access the Network Attached Storage through your network from three major operating systems, Windows, Apple Mac, and from a Chromebook.

Depending on the apps you have installed, connecting to the NAS from your tablet or smartphone is simply a matter of modifying the steps below to accommodate your mobile software.

FROM A CHROMEBOOK:

I love my Chromebooks, but I have to admit they don't hold much data on those tiny little internal drives. The OMV NAS is the perfect solution!

Open the File Browser app and click the "Three-Dot Menu" in the upper-right. Move down to "Add new service" and select "SMB file share."

The "Three-Dot" Menu and "Add New Service"

Next, a dialog window "Add File Share" appears. After following the instructions above, I see the following, with my shared drive appearing on the drop-down list. I choose that device and leave the other settings at their defaults. If you created a user name and password for the share, you should enter it in the appropriate fields:

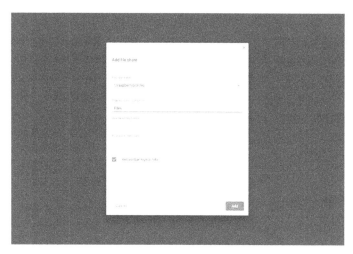

The ChromeOS Network Login Page

After clicking "Add" at the bottom, a new location is added to the Files App. It appears in the left pane at the bottom. In my case, it's located right below Google Drive, and is named "Files," since that's what we used as a name:

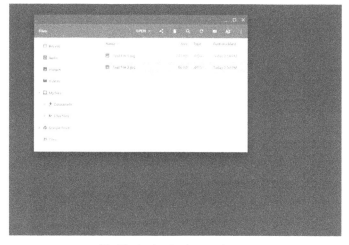

The File App showing the network Drive

And now this file location works just like a local file folder would. Drag and drop images, music, or anything else into it, and it's transparently copied to the OMV NAS server and stored there, inside the "Files" directory/folder. You can create new folders and store anything you want inside them, creating complex folder hierarchies and hundreds of thousands of files, just as you could on a local hard drive.

FROM A MAC:

1. Open a Finder window.
2. On the main menu, click on "Go" and then "Connect to server..." which will bring up the following dialog box:

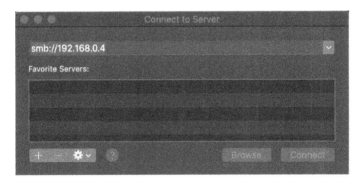

The "Connect to server..." dialog box

1. In the box, type smb://192.168.0.4 , substituting your IP address as usual.
2. You will get a second dialog box asking if you want to log in as a "Guest" or as a "Registered user." You should choose "Registered User" and then type in the user name you created to match the share you

want to connect to. Similarly, enter the appropriate password for that account.

3. If you have created multiple shares on the OMV NAS, you will next need to choose which one to connect to. Note that all users can see this list, but they can only access the share you gave them permissions for.

4. Now you should see a Finder window with your shares, and inside each of those shares are the files and folder you've put into them.

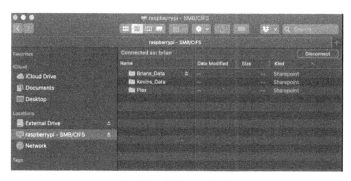

The Network Shares in Finder

And that's it! You can copy and paste, drag and drop, or do anything you would do with a local file folder at this point. Keep in mind that file transfers are going to be slower than those going to a local drive, but otherwise, there's no procedural difference.

FROM WINDOWS:

1. Open a File Explorer window.
2. In the left-hand pane, click on "Network." At some point, you will get a system notification/message to "Enable

Network Discovery." You will need to click through the prompts to turn this on.

3. Once Network Discovery has been enabled, you should see the device "RASPBERRYPI" (Or whatever you called your server) show up on the list under "Networks" like the screenshot below.

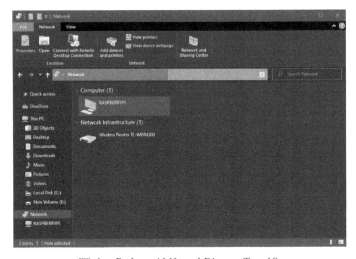

Windows Explorer with Network Discovery Turned On

4. Once the device appears, double-click on it to open the drive. You will be prompted to enter your username and password for the OMV share:

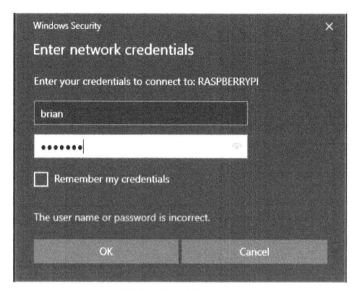

Windows Network Login Screen

5. It's going to make your life easier if you check "Remember my credentials," but keep in mind that anyone who can get access to your computer will also be able to access the network, so be advised. If in doubt, just enter your name and password manually when you need your NAS.

6. Click "OK," and then you can drag and drop, copy, move, delete, or otherwise access your files over the network, just as if they were on your local machine!

BULK COPYING FILES

The one important thing we haven't spoken about is "how do you get those files onto the hard drive we set up?"

Most of the time, you will connect to the NAS using the networking options shown in the previous sections. This is pretty much user-transparent, as it's just like copying files and folders from one location to another on your computer system. This is the simplest and easiest way to use the drive in the future, but it may not be desirable for bulk-copying potentially hundreds of thousands of files. Sometimes you have an entire hard drive worth of data to "dump" into your NAS initially. You can still use the previous section's instructions to do this, but there are three poten-tially faster ways:

1. Copy files directly from one hard drive to the NAS drive(s).
2. Drag and drop the files from your regular computer through the GUI (Finder, Explorer, etc.)
3. Use an FTP app from a "regular" computer to transfer files..

MANUAL COPY FROM THE COMMAND LINE

You can copy files to a USB drive and copy them manually to the hard drive from the command line using the cp command. This way is *not* recommended because it's cumbersome, easy to mistype something, and can be confusing about the mount point for the usb drive. It's just not the easiest way.

To begin, type the following from a terminal app:

```
sudo fdisk -l
```

This will list all the hard drives attached to your system. You should be able to tell from the size of the hard drive and other information listed as to what the system calls the new drive. If you already had sda and sdb attached, the new drive will **likely** be sdc, but you need to check and verify this, as you cannot be sure.

```
mkdir /mnt/usbdrive
```

This creates a "mount point" for the hard drive, which is essentially the path that you will use for accessing the drive.

```
sudo mount /dev/sdc1 /mnt/usbdrive
```

This connects the physical hard drive to the mount point we just created. Now, you can access your hard drive by performing action on /mnt/usbdrive

```
cd /mnt/usbdrive
ls -all
```

will move you to the root directory of the hard drive and

give you a file listing. Then, to actually copy a file, you can use the Linux "file copy" command, cp, as follows:

```
cp /mnt/usbdrive/sourcefile.txt /destina-
tion_folder/subfolder
```

you type the `cp` command followed by the full path name of the source file and the fill path where you want it copied. For a more realistic example to copy a movie file onto your NAS hard drive:

```
cp /mnt/usbdrive/Movie.avi
/mydrive/Brians_Data
```

or to copy an entire folder:

```
cp "/mnt/usbdrive/Land of the Lost" "/my-
drive/TV/Land of the Lost"
```

Note that quotation marks are required if any part of the filename or folder name contains spaces.

As you can see, this method of copying files may be fine if you have just a few files to copy, but there are easier ways!

USING A TEXT-MODE FILE MANAGER

A far easier approach than copying the files manually is to use a text-mode file manager like Midnight Commander. Midnight Commander is a visual file manager that you can install with the following commands:

```
sudo apt install mc
```

And then run the app by typing **mc** at the command line.

Note that you *still* have to create a mount point and mount the disk as in the previous section.

That said, the act of copying files with mc is much easier than typing the cp commands from the command line, but the Midnight Commander program has a million little features, and it may be a challenge in its own right. I do recommend that you install and play around with it. It's really useful for renaming, deleting, and moving files around your system later on if the need arises. Notice the bottom line of the screen shows help for using the function keys:

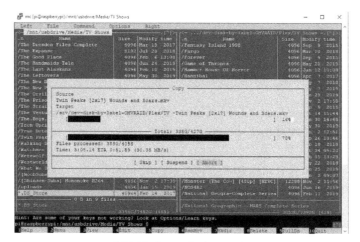

Midnight Commander Copying Files

USE FILEZILLA FROM ANOTHER COMPUTER

From another computer, you can use a graphical FTP (*File Transfer Protocol*) program to copy files to the Raspberry Pi's hard drive from somewhere else on your home network. Since it's done through your network, it's going to be a little slower than copying files directly from a USB drive.

1. First, download and install the FileZilla app on another computer on your network; the app is available in versions for

Windows, Mac, and Linux, so whatever you have, you should be able to find a working version of it. The app and installation instructions can be found at:

`https://filezilla-project.org/`

FileZilla Website

2. Once you have installed FileZilla, run it. You'll see the main window of the app, looking something like this:

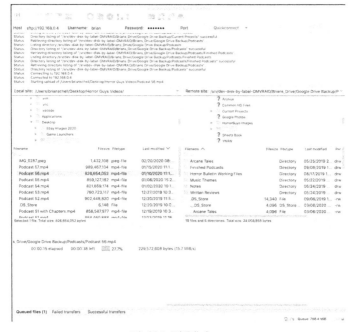

The Main FileZilla Screen

There's a lot here that we don't need to know right away, but you can look at the various options and learn the app fully if you want later on. For now, all we need to do is use FileZilla to log into the Raspberry Pi. At the top of the app's window, just below the main toolbar, are little input fields where you can type in:

- **Host:** This is your OMV Server's IP address. In the screenshot below, mine is at **192.168.0.4**; yours will vary.
- **Username:** This is the user "**pi**" unless you used something else.
- **Password:** This is whatever you changed it to earlier. If you are still using the default password (shame on you!) the default is "**raspberry**."

- **Port:** The port number is 22

Here's mine filled in:

FileZilla Login Bar

The password field doesn't display when you type it in, so be careful that you typed it correctly. Hit Enter on the keyboard or click on the "Quickconnect" button. Assuming everything is correct, you should see something like this:

The Panes of a FileZilla Window

For the moment, ignore the top and bottom panes. The four windows on the left and right sides are what's important right now.

The top-left window is the folder/directory structure on your local computer. You use this window to browse to wherever your data files are currently stored. This could be your Downloads folder, your Photo or Music Folder, somewhere on an external drive, the cloud, or wherever you put your media files. Once you point this window to the proper folder, the files within that folder will appear in the window just beneath it.

The top-right window is the same thing, but for the folders on your Raspberry Pi NAS. Move through the folders in the top window until the destination folder is visible (if you right-click, you can create, rename, and delete folders). At least in the beginning, there probably won't be any files in the destination folder.

If you see a file in the lower-left window that you want to copy to the OMV server, then you can either double-click it or drag it to the window on the right. You can watch the status of the transfer in the window on the bottom of the app. If you right-click on a file in the left-hand pane, you can rename it, delete it, add it to an upload queue, or a host of other options that you can figure out later if you choose.

This is not a book on FileZilla, but keep in mind there are many other functions that you may want to learn if you are going to be using the app a lot. You can select and add more than one file or folder at a time, you can set up a transfer queue that will run without you needing to be present, and you can set up the "Site Manager" so that you don't have to enter login information every time you load FileZilla. For the Site Manager, just pull down the File Menu and choose "Site Manager." You'll see something like this:

FileZilla Site Manager Setup Page

You can create a "New Site" on the left, then enter your login information on the right, and in the future you can use it to connect without all that typing. It's very handy. I strongly recommend spending some time and learning what FileZilla can do-- I spend a lot of time transferring files with it, and if you do any kind of "other networking stuff" at all, it can quickly become indispensable.

The next job is the time-consuming one: copy all your data files to the OMV folders you already set up.

As before, in your browser's URL bar, you can type: **http://192.168.0.4** to log into the Openmediavault server.

YOUR BACK-UP PLAN

BACKING UP YOUR SD CARD

By this point, you've put a lot of work into getting your Raspberry Pi computer all set up. You've got software installed and you have one or more external drives configured. You've built an OMV system with potentially hundreds of thousands of files. As the old movie gangsters would say, "It'd be a shame if something happened to it..."

Hard drives are pretty reliable, and you've already got all your important data files on an external hard drive. In this case, the weak point is the SD card with the operating system and all that OMV configuration data. SD cards do tend to get corrupted from time to time. Once in a while, it's a good idea to make a backup of the SD card that contains your operating system and all the apps and configuration data stored on it. That way, if something does corrupt the card, you can just restore your configured settings and system right over it, and since your actual data files will be stored on the hard drive, nothing important will be lost.

First, there are several backup utilities that are available as OMV plug-ins. Just click on "System" in the Settings pane and then "Plugins" to see the list. There are various choices, and they all operate differently and have little documentation, so I can't help much with getting these working, but be aware that they are available.

MANUAL BACK-UPS

I generally prefer a manual backup. You know it's being done because you are starting the process yourself. On the downside, you have to actually remember to *do* it! To back up the SD card, you will once again need another computer, along with whatever adaptor you may need to plug the SD card into it.

Shutdown your Raspberry Pi using the shutdown command from within the OMV web interface. When everything stops, turn off the power to the Pi. Next, remove the SD card, and move to your computer for the next steps.

FROM A MAC:

From a Mac, you must type a few commands into the terminal to backup your SD card:

1. Bring up a terminal window, but do not plug in the SD card yet.

2. Type: `diskutil list`

3. Insert the SD card.

4. Now type that same command again:

`diskutil list`

and note the new drive name that appears. This is the SD Card name/number.

5. In the terminal, type the following, replacing the x in

rdiskx with whatever the disk number is that you found in step 4:

```
sudo dd if=/dev/rdiskx of=./backup_file.dmg
```

Note that the "`if=`" parameter is for the **input file** and "`of=`" is the **output file**. That makes it a little easier to avoid getting mixed up.

6. This can take a very long time (My card took nearly an hour), and there is no feedback from the program until it's completely finished. Be patient!

SOMEDAY, IF YOU NEED TO RESTORE THE CARD:

1. Figure out the disk number by repeating steps 1-4 above.
2. Type the following three lines, replacing the *x* in *rdiskx* with whatever your SD card's drive is called:

```
diskutil unmountDisk /dev/rdiskx
```

```
sudo dd if=./backup_file.dmg of=/dev/rdiskx
```

```
sudo diskutil eject /dev/rdiskx
```

FROM WINDOWS:

Backing up the SD card from Windows is an easy process, but once again, we need to download an external app to make it happen:

1. Download and install the **Win32DiskImager** App from the link below (it's all one long line):

```
https://sourceforge.net/projects/
win32diskimager/files/latest/download
```

2. Insert the SD Card.

3. Run Win32DiskImager, and then choose both the location where you want to create the backup file and the name of the SD card.

4. Click "Read" to begin copying.

5. This can take a very long time, but you can watch progress bar as shown in Figure 2-3

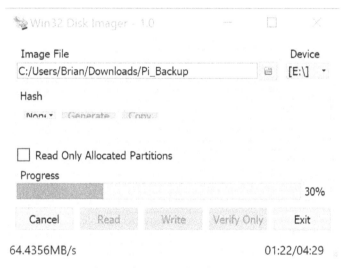

Win32DiskImager Reading the SD Card

If, at some point, you need to restore the SD card from your backup, just run Win32DiskImager, choose the backup file and the SD Card drive letter, and choose "Write" instead of "Read" in the steps above to run the process in reverse.

BACKING UP YOUR HARD DRIVE(S)

Just like with Windows or Macs, there are various ways to backup your hard drives. The simplest way to backup your external hard drive is to simply:

1. Shutdown your Raspberry Pi
2. Unplug the hard drive
3. Plug the drive into another computer
4. Copy or backup the drive with whatever backup software you're already familiar with.

It's also possible to plug in yet another external hard drive and mirror your data drive to that new drive using the *dd* command. If you go back to the section where we installed your first hard drive, you can once again use the `sudo fdisk -l` command with the list (L menu option) to view all the attached drive names. You already know the drive name of your media drive (in our earlier example, it was `/dev/sda1`). You will also need to plug in and figure out the drive name of the blank, target drive (possibly `/dev/sdb1`, but it could be something else). Once you know the two drive/partition names, you can use the dd command like this:

```
sudo dd if=<input device name> of=<output
device name>
```

Substituting your drive names for the source and destination drives. For example, if your working NAS drive is `sda1`, and your backup drive is `sdb1`, then you would type:

```
sudo dd if=/dev/sda1 of=/dev/sdb1
```

Note that one, only partially joking, name for the dd

command is "disk destroyer." If you get the two drive names backwards, it'll overwrite your media with whatever's on the second drive, which is definitely **not** what you want. Be very careful with this command.

More information can be found at:

```
https://opensource.com/article/18/7/how-
use-dd-linux
```

Another option is to use a command line file manager like Midnight Commander to copy files more visually.

TROUBLESHOOTING CHECKLIST

There were a lot of steps involved in setting up Openmedi-avault, and it's easy to skip over a line or miss a whole command somewhere. Here's an overview of the entire process to speed you along on your second system or to help you debug something that's going wrong.

SETTING UP THE RASPBERRY PI

1. Buy the various parts
2. Download the Raspbian operating system
3. Flash Raspbian onto the MicroSD card using Etcher
4. Create the blank "ssh" file on the MicroSD card
5. Assemble all the pieces
6. Plug into Ethernet
7. Turn it on

NETWORKING AND LINUX SETUP

1. Find your Raspberry Pi's IP Address on the network by either looking at your router's "admin screen" or using an app like "Angry IP Scanner."
2. Download and install a terminal app on your other computer.
3. Use ssh to connect to the Pi remotely. (*ssh username@ipnumber*)
4. Log in for the first time. (*user: pi / password: raspberry*)
5. Change the password for the user Pi.
6. Update the operating system (sudo apt update then sudo apt upgrade)
7. Reboot the system with sudo reboot
8. Download and install Openmediavault (*see main text*)

SINGLE HARD DRIVE SETUP

1. Shutdown/power off the system, plug in the hard drive, and power the system back on.
2. "Wipe" the disk.
3. Create a file system on the hard drive.
4. Mount the drive
5. Use "Access Rights Management" to "Add shared folder."
6. Set up multiple users, accounts, and groups as detailed below.
7. Go to "Services>SMB/CIFS" and enable SMB/CIFS.

RAID SETUP

1. Setup the Raspberry Pi and connect two blank drives.
2. Find out the names of the two drives (i.e. */dev/sda* and */dev/sdb*).
3. Go to "Services>SMB/CIFS" and disable SMB/CIFS.
4. Connect to the Pi with the terminal app from another computer.
5. Verify that the system can "see" both blank drives.
6. Type in the command line command to create the RAID array. When this command is finally complete, the two drives will appear to be one single drive (It's mirroring).
7. Wait a long time. My example system literally took 18 hours.
8. Create a file system on the single RAID device (takes around 1 hour).
9. Mount the RAID drive.
10. Use "Access Rights Management" to "Add shared folder."
11. Set up multiple users, accounts, and groups as detailed below.
12. Create a shared folder.
13. Go to "Services>SMB/CIFS" and enable SMB/CIFS.

SET UP MULTIPLE USERS

1. Under "Access Rights Management>Users," use the "Add" button to create a user account.

2. Under "Access Rights Management>Groups," use the "Add" button to create a group with the same name as the user account.

3. Under "Access Rights Management>Shared folders," use the "Add" button to create a folder for each user.

4. Under "Access Rights Management>Shared folders," use the "Privileges" button to assign the user to his/her own folder.

5. Under "Access Rights Management>Shared folders>ACL," assign the appropriate groups to that user's folder.

6. Under "Services>SMB/CIFS," verify that the "Inherit ACLs/Honor existing ACLs" switch is turned on.

UPGRADES

OK, so we've gotten everything assembled, configured, and working just fine. Where can we go from here?

1. There are various plugins and extras that can add functionality to Openmediavault. Some of these are very technical and may not appeal to the typical NAS user, but it's worth taking a look at what's available before you dismiss the idea out of hand. These can be found in the Setting pane under "Plugins" and "OMV-Extras."

2. You can easily add more hard drives to the system by repeating the steps given in this book. The first drive is /dev/sda, the second is /dev/sdb, and a third would be /dev/sdc, and so forth. You have four USB ports on the Raspberry Pi, and there's absolutely no reason you can't have four drives plugged in. You could plug in more than that using a USB hub, but there is a performance hit with that, so I would suggest four drives as a practical limitation.

3. You can expand the Raspberry Pi itself. There are expansion boards for the Pi called "hats" which sit on top of the Pi motherboard and offer various kinds of hardware expansion. For a NAS, the one I would recommend looking at is the "SATA hat." If you have some kind of powered enclosure that accepts multiple hard drives, you can use this hat to plug in up to four internal hard drives. You can use an old PC case and power supply to house the hard drives, and then use the Pi to be the brains of the system. My own feeling on this is that if you need that much more computing power, it may be time to give up on the Pi and just use a full-sized PC, but your mileage may vary on this.

4. Eventually, you might find yourself outgrowing the Raspberry Pi. You can use the same software procedures given in this book to install Ubuntu Linux (rather than Raspbian) on a regular PC and use that to control your NAS if desired. Raspbian is mostly a scaled-down version of the Ubuntu Linux operating system for the PC, so all the commands we've outlined here will work on an Ubuntu system. You can fit a LOT of hard drives inside some computer cases! Again, the Raspberry Pi is fine for most people, but if you need more than four drives attached, this may be the best solution.

CONCLUSION

And that is about all there is to it. Openmediavault is continually adding new features and settings, so I haven't gone into the weeds too much on some of the more technical settings. What we've covered here will get you set up and running, but there's still quite a bit of fine-tuning and customizing that you can do. There are plugins, extras, and Docker containers, as well as multiple different drive configurations you can choose from.

The two setups I've described in this book (single drive and dual-drive RAID) are only a couple of the possibilities. Part of the fun of doing this all yourself is that now that you have a basic working system, you can experiment with it. Of course, you shouldn't experiment with your working, live system, but Raspberry Pis are so inexpensive that it isn't a huge stretch to get a spare one for "messing around" with settings.

And of course, the heart of the system is the Raspberry Pi, the tiny little inexpensive computer. The Raspberry Pi as a device has come a long way in just a few short years. Once just a device for electronics nerds, now it's a full, completely usable computer for many types of projects that once required a full-sized PC.

The Openmediavault server is just one of a vast number of open-source projects for which you can use these little devices. Many people use a Raspberry Pi for one project, for example, a NAS server, and then end up getting more of them for other things, like a home Plex Media Server, a music jukebox, "Magic Mirror," and hundreds of other applications, not to mention as a complete desktop replacement. If this last idea intrigues you, I should point out that I have also written "Computing with the Raspberry Pi: Command Line and GUI Linux (Technology in Action)" available through Apress Publishing, which is all about using the Pi as a desktop replacement. You can do it!

Good luck with your Pi, and have loads of fun with your Openmediavault NAS Server!

ABOUT THE AUTHOR

I am a former College IT Instructor with an extensive back-ground in computers dating back to the 1980s. Currently, I write on a wide array of topics from computers, to world religions, to ham radio, and I've even released an occasional short horror tale.

———

I'd love to hear your stories of success and failure with the Raspberry Pi and Openmediavault server software. If there's something you would like to see in a future edition of the book, or otherwise have suggestions, please drop me a note.

Contact me at:

Web: http://BrianSchell.com
Email: brian@brianschell.com

Also, please join my email update list— There's NO weekly SPAM or filler material, only announcements of new books or major updates.

Email update link: http://brianschell.com/list/

If you have a suggestion or find a mistake, email me about

it, and I'll get it into an updated edition of the book. Got a gripe, complaint, question, or just adoring fan mail? Same thing!

LEAVE A REVIEW

If this book helped you, please leave a review where you purchased this book. Reviews are the best way to help out!

SHARE WITH YOUR FRIENDS

Did you enjoy this book? Please use the buttons below to spread the word to your friends and followers.

twitter.com/BrianSchell
facebook.com/Brian.Schell
instagram.com/brian_schell
pinterest.com/brianschell

ALSO BY BRIAN SCHELL

Amateur Radio

• D-Star for Beginners

• Echolink for Beginners

• DMR for Beginners Using the Tytera MD-380

• SDR for Beginners with the SDRPlay

• Programming Amateur Radios with CHIRP

• FM Satellite Communications for Beginners

• Trunking Scanners for Beginners Using the Uniden TrunkTracker

Technology

• Going Chromebook: Living in the Cloud

• Building NAS Server with Raspberry Pi and Openmediavault

• Building a Plex Server with Raspberry Pi

• Computing with the Raspberry Pi: Command Line and GUI Linux (Technology in Action)

• Going Chromebook: Mastering Google Docs

• Going Chromebook: Mastering Google Sheets

• Going Text: Mastering the Power of the Command Line

• Going iPad: Ditching the Desktop

• DOS Today: Running Vintage MS-DOS Games and Apps on a Modern Computer

Old-Time Radio Listener's Guides

• OTR Listener's Guide to Dark Fantasy

• OTR Listener's Guide to Box 13

The Five-Minute Buddhist Series

• The Five-Minute Buddhist

• The Five-Minute Buddhist Returns

• The Five-Minute Buddhist Meditates

• The Five-Minute Buddhist's Quick Start Guide to Buddhism

• Teaching and Learning in Japan: An English Teacher Abroad

Fiction with Kevin L. Knights:

• Tales to Make You Shiver

• Tales to Make You Shiver 2

• Random Acts of Cloning

• Jess and the Monsters

www.ingramcontent.com/pod-product-compliance
Lightning Source LLC
LaVergne TN
LVHW041216050326
832903LV00021B/653